I0037489

©

Copyright 2022 - All rights reserved.

You may not reproduce, duplicate or send the contents of this book without direct written permission from the author. You cannot apply hereby despite any circumstance blame the publisher or hold him or her to legal responsibility for any reparation, compensations, or monetary forfeiture owing to the information included herein, either in a direct or an indirect way.

Legal Notice: This book has copyright protection. You can use the book for personal purposes. You should not sell, use, alter, distribute, quote, take excerpts, or paraphrase in part or whole the material contained in this book without obtaining the permission of the author first.

Disclaimer Notice: You must take note that the information in this document is for casual reading and entertainment purposes only. We have made every attempt to provide accurate, up-to-date, and reliable information. We do not express or imply guarantees of any kind. The persons who read admit that the writer is not occupied in giving legal, financial, medical, or other advice. We put this book content by sourcing various places.

Please consult a licensed professional before you try any techniques shown in this book. By going through this document, the book lover comes to an an agreement that under no situation is the author accountable for any forfeiture, direct or indirect, which they may incur because of the use of material contained in this document, including, but not limited to, — errors, omissions, or inaccuracies.

Personal Information	
Name:	Date of Birth:
Adress:	
Business Adress:	
Email:	
Mobile Telephone:	
Home Telephone:	
Fax:	

Emergency Contact	
Name:	Relationship:
Adress:	
Mobile Telephone:	
Home Telephone:	
Email:	

Notes

Vehicle Information	
Vehicle:	Year:
Make:	
Model:	
Engine:	
VIN Number:	
Purchase Date:	Mileage at Purchase:
Purchase Form:	

Insurance Company	
Company Name:	
Adress:	
Office:	Work:
Phone:	Fax:
Email:	
Website:	
Agent:	Phone:
Cost:	
Insurance Numbre:	
Cover Details:	
Start Date:	End Date:

Notes

YEAR: ____________ MONTH: ____________ MODEL: ____________

Date / Time	Oil Changed	Air Filter	Balance Tires	Wheel Alignment	Fuel Filter	Brakes Serviced	Spark Plugs	Transmission	Wiper Blades	Batteries	Radiator	Belts&Horses	Mileage

make: date purchased:

model: purchased price:

license plate: purchased form:

Date/Time	Maintenance/Comments	Mileage

YEAR: ________ MONTH: ________ MODEL: ________

Date/Time	Oil Changed	Air Filter	Balance Tires	Wheel Alignment	Fuel Filter	Brakes Serviced	Spark Plugs	Transmission	Wiper Blades	Batteries	Radiator	Belts&Horses	Mileage

make: date purchased:

model: purchased price:

license plate: purchased form:

DATE/TIME	MAINTENANCE/COMMENTS	MILEAGE

YEAR: ________ MONTH: ________ MODEL: ________

Date/Time	Oil Changed	Air Filter	Balance Tires	Wheel Alignment	Fuel Filter	Brakes Serviced	Spark Plugs	Transmission	Wiper Blades	Batteries	Radiator	Belts&Horses	Mileage

make: date purchased:

model: purchased price:

license plate: purchased form:

DATE/TIME	MAINTENANCE/COMMENTS	MILEAGE

YEAR: ________ MONTH: ________ MODEL: ________

Date/Time	Oil Changed	Air Filter	Balance Tires	Wheel Alignment	Fuel Filter	Brakes Serviced	Spark Plugs	Transmission	Wiper Blades	Batteries	Radiator	Belts&Horses	Mileage

make: date purchased:

model: purchased price:

license plate: purchased form:

DATE/TIME	MAINTENANCE/COMMENTS	MILEAGE

YEAR: ____________ MONTH: ____________ MODEL: ____________

Date/Time	Oil Changed	Air Filter	Balance Tires	Wheel Alignment	Fuel Filter	Brakes Serviced	Spark Plugs	Transmission	Wiper Blades	Batteries	Radiator	Belts&Horses	Mileage

make: date purchased:

model: purchased price:

license plate: purchased form:

DATE/TIME	MAINTENANCE/COMMENTS	MILEAGE

YEAR: ________ MONTH: ________ MODEL: ________

Date/Time	Oil Changed	Air Filter	Balance Tires	Wheel Alignment	Fuel Filter	Brakes Serviced	Spark Plugs	Transmission	Wiper Blades	Batteries	Radiator	Belts&Horses	Mileage

make: date purchased:

model: purchased price:

license plate: purchased form:

Date/Time	Maintenance/Comments	Mileage

YEAR: ________ MONTH: ________ MODEL: ________

Date/Time	Oil Changed	Air Filter	Balance Tires	Wheel Alignment	Fuel Filter	Brakes Serviced	Spark Plugs	Transmission	Wiper Blades	Batteries	Radiator	Belts&Horses	Mileage

make: date purchased:

model: purchased price:

license plate: purchased form:

Date/Time	Maintenance/Comments	Mileage

YEAR: __________ MONTH: __________ MODEL: __________

Date/Time	Oil Changed	Air Filter	Balance Tires	Wheel Alignment	Fuel Filter	Brakes Serviced	Spark Plugs	Transmission	Wiper Blades	Batteries	Radiator	Belts&Horses	Mileage

make: date purchased:

model: purchased price:

license plate: purchased form:

Date/Time	Maintenance/Comments	Mileage

YEAR: ____________ MONTH: ____________ MODEL: ____________

Date / Time	Oil Changed	Air Filter	Balance Tires	Wheel Alignment	Fuel Filter	Brakes Serviced	Spark Plugs	Transmission	Wiper Blades	Batteries	Radiator	Belts&Horses	Mileage

make: date purchased:

model: purchased price:

license plate: purchased form:

DATE/TIME	MAINTENANCE/COMMENTS	MILEAGE

YEAR: ________ MONTH: ________ MODEL: ________

Date / Time	Oil Changed	Air Filter	Balance Tires	Wheel Alignment	Fuel Filter	Brakes Serviced	Spark Plugs	Transmission	Wiper Blades	Batteries	Radiator	Belts&Horses	Mileage

make: date purchased:

model: purchased price:

license plate: purchased form:

Date/Time	Maintenance/Comments	Mileage

YEAR: ________ MONTH: ________ MODEL: ________

Date/Time	Oil Changed	Air Filter	Balance Tires	Wheel Alignment	Fuel Filter	Brakes Serviced	Spark Plugs	Transmission	Wiper Blades	Batteries	Radiator	Belts&Horses	Mileage

make:

date purchased:

model:

purchased price:

license plate:

purchased form:

DATE/TIME	MAINTENANCE/COMMENTS	MILEAGE

YEAR: __________ MONTH: __________ MODEL: __________

Date/Time	Oil Changed	Air Filter	Balance Tires	Wheel Alignment	Fuel Filter	Brakes Serviced	Spark Plugs	Transmission	Wiper Blades	Batteries	Radiator	Belts&Horses	Mileage

make:

date purchased:

model:

purchased price:

license plate:

purchased form:

DATE/TIME	MAINTENANCE/COMMENTS	MILEAGE

YEAR: __________ MONTH: __________ MODEL: __________

Date / Time	Oil Changed	Air Filter	Balance Tires	Wheel Alignment	Fuel Filter	Brakes Serviced	Spark Plugs	Transmission	Wiper Blades	Batteries	Radiator	Belts&Horses	Mileage

make: date purchased:

model: purchased price:

license plate: purchased form:

Date/Time	Maintenance/Comments	Mileage

YEAR: __________ MONTH: __________ MODEL: __________

Date/Time	Oil Changed	Air Filter	Balance Tires	Wheel Alignment	Fuel Filter	Brakes Serviced	Spark Plugs	Transmission	Wiper Blades	Batteries	Radiator	Belts&Horses	Mileage

make:

date purchased:

model:

purchased price:

license plate:

purchased form:

DATE/TIME	MAINTENANCE/COMMENTS	MILEAGE

YEAR: ____________ MONTH: ____________ MODEL: ____________

Date / Time	Oil Changed	Air Filter	Balance Tires	Wheel Alignment	Fuel Filter	Brakes Serviced	Spark Plugs	Transmission	Wiper Blades	Batteries	Radiator	Belts&Horses	Mileage

make: date purchased:

model: purchased price:

license plate: purchased form:

Date/Time	Maintenance/Comments	Mileage

YEAR: __________ MONTH: __________ MODEL: __________

Date/Time	Oil Changed	Air Filter	Balance Tires	Wheel Alignment	Fuel Filter	Brakes Serviced	Spark Plugs	Transmission	Wiper Blades	Batteries	Radiator	Belts&Horses	Mileage

make: date purchased:

model: purchased price:

license plate: purchased form:

Date/Time	Maintenance/Comments	Mileage

YEAR: ____________ MONTH: ____________ MODEL: ____________

Date/Time	Oil Changed	Air Filter	Balance Tires	Wheel Alignment	Fuel Filter	Brakes Serviced	Spark Plugs	Transmission	Wiper Blades	Batteries	Radiator	Belts&Horses	Mileage

make: date purchased:

model: purchased price:

license plate: purchased form:

DATE/TIME	MAINTENANCE/COMMENTS	MILEAGE

YEAR: ________ MONTH: ________ MODEL: ________

Date / Time	Oil Changed	Air Filter	Balance Tires	Wheel Alignment	Fuel Filter	Brakes Serviced	Spark Plugs	Transmission	Wiper Blades	Batteries	Radiator	Belts&Horses	Mileage

make:

date purchased:

model:

purchased price:

license plate:

purchased form:

Date/Time	Maintenance/Comments	Mileage

YEAR: __________ MONTH: __________ MODEL: __________

Date/Time	Oil Changed	Air Filter	Balance Tires	Wheel Alignment	Fuel Filter	Brakes Serviced	Spark Plugs	Transmission	Wiper Blades	Batteries	Radiator	Belts&Horses	Mileage

make:

date purchased:

model:

purchased price:

license plate:

purchased form:

DATE/TIME	MAINTENANCE/COMMENTS	MILEAGE

YEAR: ________ MONTH: ________ MODEL: ________

Date / Time	Oil Changed	Air Filter	Balance Tires	Wheel Alignment	Fuel Filter	Brakes Serviced	Spark Plugs	Transmission	Wiper Blades	Batteries	Radiator	Belts&Horses	Mileage

make: date purchased:

model: purchased price:

license plate: purchased form:

Date/Time	Maintenance/Comments	Mileage

YEAR: ________ MONTH: ________ MODEL: ________

Date / Time	Oil Changed	Air Filter	Balance Tires	Wheel Alignment	Fuel Filter	Brakes Serviced	Spark Plugs	Transmission	Wiper Blades	Batteries	Radiator	Belts&Horses	Mileage

make:

date purchased:

model:

purchased price:

license plate:

purchased form:

Date/Time	Maintenance/Comments	Mileage

YEAR: ________ MONTH: ________ MODEL: ________

Date / Time	Oil Changed	Air Filter	Balance Tires	Wheel Alignment	Fuel Filter	Brakes Serviced	Spark Plugs	Transmission	Wiper Blades	Batteries	Radiator	Belts&Horses	Mileage

make: date purchased:

model: purchased price:

license plate: purchased form:

Date/Time	Maintenance/Comments	Mileage

YEAR: __________ MONTH: __________ MODEL: __________

Date/Time	Oil Changed	Air Filter	Balance Tires	Wheel Alignment	Fuel Filter	Brakes Serviced	Spark Plugs	Transmission	Wiper Blades	Batteries	Radiator	Belts&Horses	Mileage

make: date purchased:

model: purchased price:

license plate: purchased form:

DATE/TIME	MAINTENANCE/COMMENTS	MILEAGE

YEAR: ________ MONTH: ________ MODEL: ________

Date/Time	Oil Changed	Air Filter	Balance Tires	Wheel Alignment	Fuel Filter	Brakes Serviced	Spark Plugs	Transmission	Wiper Blades	Batteries	Radiator	Belts&Horses	Mileage

make:

date purchased:

model:

purchased price:

license plate:

purchased form:

DATE/TIME	MAINTENANCE/COMMENTS	MILEAGE

YEAR: __________ MONTH: __________ MODEL: __________

Date/Time	Oil Changed	Air Filter	Balance Tires	Wheel Alignment	Fuel Filter	Brakes Serviced	Spark Plugs	Transmission	Wiper Blades	Batteries	Radiator	Belts&Horses	Mileage

make: date purchased:

model: purchased price:

license plate: purchased form:

DATE/TIME	MAINTENANCE/COMMENTS	MILEAGE

YEAR: ________ MONTH: ________ MODEL: ________

Date/Time	Oil Changed	Air Filter	Balance Tires	Wheel Alignment	Fuel Filter	Brakes Serviced	Spark Plugs	Transmission	Wiper Blades	Batteries	Radiator	Belts&Horses	Mileage

make:

date purchased:

model:

purchased price:

license plate:

purchased form:

DATE/TIME	MAINTENANCE/COMMENTS	MILEAGE

YEAR: __________ MONTH: __________ MODEL: __________

Date/Time	Oil Changed	Air Filter	Balance Tires	Wheel Alignment	Fuel Filter	Brakes Serviced	Spark Plugs	Transmission	Wiper Blades	Batteries	Radiator	Belts&Horses	Mileage

make: date purchased:

model: purchased price:

license plate: purchased form:

Date/Time	Maintenance/Comments	Mileage

YEAR: __________ MONTH: __________ MODEL: __________

Date/Time	Oil Changed	Air Filter	Balance Tires	Wheel Alignment	Fuel Filter	Brakes Serviced	Spark Plugs	Transmission	Wiper Blades	Batteries	Radiator	Belts&Horses	Mileage

make: date purchased:

model: purchased price:

license plate: purchased form:

DATE/TIME	MAINTENANCE/COMMENTS	MILEAGE

YEAR: __________ MONTH: __________ MODEL: __________

Date/Time	Oil Changed	Air Filter	Balance Tires	Wheel Alignment	Fuel Filter	Brakes Serviced	Spark Plugs	Transmission	Wiper Blades	Batteries	Radiator	Belts&Horses	Mileage

make:

date purchased:

model:

purchased price:

license plate:

purchased form:

DATE/TIME	MAINTENANCE/COMMENTS	MILEAGE

YEAR: ____________ MONTH: ____________ MODEL: ____________

Date/Time	Oil Changed	Air Filter	Balance Tires	Wheel Alignment	Fuel Filter	Brakes Serviced	Spark Plugs	Transmission	Wiper Blades	Batteries	Radiator	Belts&Horses	Mileage

make:

date purchased:

model:

purchased price:

license plate:

purchased form:

Date/Time	Maintenance/Comments	Mileage

YEAR: ________ MONTH: ________ MODEL: ________

Date/Time	Oil Changed	Air Filter	Balance Tires	Wheel Alignment	Fuel Filter	Brakes Serviced	Spark Plugs	Transmission	Wiper Blades	Batteries	Radiator	Belts&Horses	Mileage

make: date purchased:

model: purchased price:

license plate: purchased form:

DATE/TIME	MAINTENANCE/COMMENTS	MILEAGE

YEAR: __________ MONTH: __________ MODEL: __________

Date/Time	Oil Changed	Air Filter	Balance Tires	Wheel Alignment	Fuel Filter	Brakes Serviced	Spark Plugs	Transmission	Wiper Blades	Batteries	Radiator	Belts&Horses	Mileage

make: date purchased:

model: purchased price:

license plate: purchased form:

DATE/TIME	MAINTENANCE/COMMENTS	MILEAGE

YEAR: ________ MONTH: ________ MODEL: ________

Date/Time	Oil Changed	Air Filter	Balance Tires	Wheel Alignment	Fuel Filter	Brakes Serviced	Spark Plugs	Transmission	Wiper Blades	Batteries	Radiator	Belts&Horses	Mileage

make:

date purchased:

model:

purchased price:

license plate:

purchased form:

Date/Time	Maintenance/Comments	Mileage

YEAR: __________ MONTH: __________ MODEL: __________

Date / Time	Oil Changed	Air Filter	Balance Tires	Wheel Alignment	Fuel Filter	Brakes Serviced	Spark Plugs	Transmission	Wiper Blades	Batteries	Radiator	Belts&Horses	Mileage

make: date purchased:

model: purchased price:

license plate: purchased form:

DATE/TIME	MAINTENANCE/COMMENTS	MILEAGE

YEAR: ____________ MONTH: ____________ MODEL: ____________

Date / Time	Oil Changed	Air Filter	Balance Tires	Wheel Alignment	Fuel Filter	Brakes Serviced	Spark Plugs	Transmission	Wiper Blades	Batteries	Radiator	Belts&Horses	Mileage

make: date purchased:

model: purchased price:

license plate: purchased form:

DATE/TIME	MAINTENANCE/COMMENTS	MILEAGE

YEAR: ________ MONTH: ________ MODEL: ________

Date/Time	Oil Changed	Air Filter	Balance Tires	Wheel Alignment	Fuel Filter	Brakes Serviced	Spark Plugs	Transmission	Wiper Blades	Batteries	Radiator	Belts&Horses	Mileage

make: date purchased:

model: purchased price:

license plate: purchased form:

DATE/TIME	MAINTENANCE/COMMENTS	MILEAGE

YEAR: ____________ MONTH: ____________ MODEL: ____________

Date/Time	Oil Changed	Air Filter	Balance Tires	Wheel Alignment	Fuel Filter	Brakes Serviced	Spark Plugs	Transmission	Wiper Blades	Batteries	Radiator	Belts&Horses	Mileage

make: date purchased:

model: purchased price:

license plate: purchased form:

Date/Time	Maintenance/Comments	Mileage

YEAR: __________ MONTH: __________ MODEL: __________

Date/Time	Oil Changed	Air Filter	Balance Tires	Wheel Alignment	Fuel Filter	Brakes Serviced	Spark Plugs	Transmission	Wiper Blades	Batteries	Radiator	Belts&Horses	Mileage

make:

date purchased:

model:

purchased price:

license plate:

purchased form:

DATE/TIME	MAINTENANCE/COMMENTS	MILEAGE

YEAR: ________ MONTH: ________ MODEL: ________

Date/Time	Oil Changed	Air Filter	Balance Tires	Wheel Alignment	Fuel Filter	Brakes Serviced	Spark Plugs	Transmission	Wiper Blades	Batteries	Radiator	Belts&Horses	Mileage

make: date purchased:

model: purchased price:

license plate: purchased form:

DATE/TIME	MAINTENANCE/COMMENTS	MILEAGE

YEAR: __________ MONTH: __________ MODEL: __________

Date/Time	Oil Changed	Air Filter	Balance Tires	Wheel Alignment	Fuel Filter	Brakes Serviced	Spark Plugs	Transmission	Wiper Blades	Batteries	Radiator	Belts&Horses	Mileage

make: date purchased:

model: purchased price:

license plate: purchased form:

DATE/TIME	MAINTENANCE/COMMENTS	MILEAGE

YEAR: ____________ MONTH: ____________ MODEL: ____________

Date/Time	Oil Changed	Air Filter	Balance Tires	Wheel Alignment	Fuel Filter	Brakes Serviced	Spark Plugs	Transmission	Wiper Blades	Batteries	Radiator	Belts&Horses	Mileage

make: date purchased:

model: purchased price:

license plate: purchased form:

DATE/TIME	MAINTENANCE/COMMENTS	MILEAGE

YEAR: ________ MONTH: ________ MODEL: ________

Date/Time	Oil Changed	Air Filter	Balance Tires	Wheel Alignment	Fuel Filter	Brakes Serviced	Spark Plugs	Transmission	Wiper Blades	Batteries	Radiator	Belts&Horses	Mileage

make: date purchased:

model: purchased price:

license plate: purchased form:

Date/Time	Maintenance/Comments	Mileage

YEAR: ______ MONTH: ______ MODEL: ______

Date/Time	Oil Changed	Air Filter	Balance Tires	Wheel Alignment	Fuel Filter	Brakes Serviced	Spark Plugs	Transmission	Wiper Blades	Batteries	Radiator	Belts&Horses	Mileage

make:

date purchased:

model:

purchased price:

license plate:

purchased form:

Date/Time	Maintenance/Comments	Mileage

YEAR: ____________ MONTH: ____________ MODEL: ____________

Date/Time	Oil Changed	Air Filter	Balance Tires	Wheel Alignment	Fuel Filter	Brakes Serviced	Spark Plugs	Transmission	Wiper Blades	Batteries	Radiator	Belts&Horses	Mileage

make: date purchased:

model: purchased price:

license plate: purchased form:

DATE/TIME	MAINTENANCE/COMMENTS	MILEAGE

YEAR: ________ MONTH: ________ MODEL: ________

Date/Time	Oil Changed	Air Filter	Balance Tires	Wheel Alignment	Fuel Filter	Brakes Serviced	Spark Plugs	Transmission	Wiper Blades	Batteries	Radiator	Belts&Horses	Mileage

make:

date purchased:

model:

purchased price:

license plate:

purchased form:

DATE/TIME	MAINTENANCE/COMMENTS	MILEAGE

YEAR: ________ MONTH: ________ MODEL: ________

Date/Time	Oil Changed	Air Filter	Balance Tires	Wheel Alignment	Fuel Filter	Brakes Serviced	Spark Plugs	Transmission	Wiper Blades	Batteries	Radiator	Belts&Horses	Mileage

make: date purchased:

model: purchased price:

license plate: purchased form:

DATE/TIME	MAINTENANCE/COMMENTS	MILEAGE

YEAR: __________ MONTH: __________ MODEL: __________

Date / Time	Oil Changed	Air Filter	Balance Tires	Wheel Alignment	Fuel Filter	Brakes Serviced	Spark Plugs	Transmission	Wiper Blades	Batteries	Radiator	Belts&Horses	Mileage

YEARLY SUMMARY

month	total distance	total cost of fuel	total repairs	total maint.
jan				
feb				
mar				
apr				
may				
jun				
jul				
aug				
sep				
oct				
nov				
dec				

Thank you!

WE ARE GLAD THAT YOU PURCHASED OUR BOOK!
PLEASE LET US KNOW HOW WE CAN IMPROVE IT!
YOUR FEEDBACK IS ESSENTIAL TO US.

Contact us at:

log'Sin@gmail.com

JUST TITLE THE EMAIL 'CREATIVE' AND WE WILL GIVE YOU SOME EXTRA SURPRISES!